THE

MAINE

IDEA

Books by
Keith Jennison

"YUP... NOPE" & OTHER VERMONT DIALOGUES

GREEN MOUNTAINS AND ROCK RIBS

VERMONT IS WHERE YOU FIND IT

REMEMBER MAINE

THE MAINE IDEA

THE
MAINE
IDEA

Stories and Pictures arranged by

KEITH JENNISON

THE COUNTRYMAN PRESS
Woodstock, Vermont 05091

FOR LOUISE

THE
MAINE
IDEA

1

We only got two seasons up here,
July . . .

and winter.

2

Where's this road go?

Don't go nowhere, Mister;

stays right here.

3

What's the death rate around here?

About one to a person.

4

How far is it to Portland? . . . Well, it's about thirty thousand miles the way you're headed . . .

and there's some stretches of

pretty bad wheelin'.

But isn't this the Portland road?

Sure it's the Portland road, but if
I was you and if I was going to
Portland, I sure would change ends
with that car.

5

How are you, Aaron?

I'm all right, if you don't ask
for details.

6

My sister and I ain't really
lonesome out here, we got each
other to talk to,

but we need another woman to talk about.

7

How much money did you say old
man Ritchie left when he died?

All of it.

8

He didn't know about Maine.

He didn't know about the potatoes . . .

or the apples . . .

or the lobsters . . .

He said that he thought all we raised up here was big piles of manure.

So I said, "Yup, and we fertilized

your whole damned West."

9

Is it far to town?

Well, it seems farther than it is,

but you'll find out it ain't.

10

Down this way folks eat

so much seafood . . .

Their stomachs rise and fall

with the tide.

11

Our ancestors didn't come over on the *Mayflower*, but they was there to meet the boat.

12

Lew Franklin says he'd knock them crazy ideas out of his son, if he knew where to hit him.

13

When they told him about how Andy Carnegie came to this country with twenty-five cents in his pocket and died leaving a fortune of 250 million dollars, all he said was . . .

He must have had a very savin' woman.

14

My cow may be having a calf by your
bull, Mr. Madison . . .

but it ain't as though anything had been stole that could be returned.

15

My goodness, 'way out here in the country, whatever do you people do in the winter?

We don't.

16

Us country women make good wives.
No matter what happens we've seen
worse.

17

Get off your land? What makes it your land?

I got it from my father. He got it from his father, and *his* father fought the Indians for it.

All right, Mister, I'll fight you for it.

18

You don't have to be crazy to live
this far from anywhere . . .

but it helps.

19

The first winter up here you don't
believe what others tell you . . .

The second winter you don't believe
what you tell yourself.

20

You say you want a round trip ticket.

Where to?

Back here.

PICTURE CREDITS

All photographs secured through the courtesy of
R. I. Nesmith and Associates